JEWISH PRAYER

RABBI LOUIS JACOBS, B.A., Ph.D.

Minister, New West End Synagogue, London

JEWISH PRAYER

WIPF & STOCK · Eugene, Oregon

Wipf and Stock Publishers
199 W 8th Ave, Suite 3
Eugene, OR 97401

Jewish Prayer
By Jacobs, Louis
Copyright©1955 by Jacobs, Louis
ISBN 13: 978-1-60608-237-9
Publication date 10/22/2008
Previously published by Valentine Mitchell, 1955

Contents

	Page
CHAPTER I WHAT IS JEWISH PRAYER?	1
CHAPTER II DOES GOD ANSWER PRAYER?	8
CHAPTER III PRAISING GOD	17
CHAPTER IV THANKING GOD	27
CHAPTER V THE USE OF HEBREW IN PRAYER	33
CHAPTER VI THE TECHNIQUE OF PRAYER	44
CHAPTER VII CONGREGATIONAL PRAYER AND THE SYNAGOGUE	54

CHAPTER I

What is Jewish Prayer?

Prayer is a universal phenomenon in the soul-life of man. It is the soul's reaction to the terrors and joys, the uncertainties and dreams of life. "The reason why we pray," says William James, "is simply that we cannot help praying." It is an instinct that springs eternally from man's unquenchable faith in a living God, almighty and merciful, Who heareth prayer, and answereth those who call upon Him in truth; and it ranges from half-articulate petition for help in distress to highest adoration, from confession of sin to jubilant expression of joyful fellowship with God, from thanksgiving to the solemn resolve to do His will as if it were our will. Prayer is a Jacob's ladder joining earth to heaven; and, as nothing else, wakens in the children of men the sense of kinship with their Father on High. It is an "ascent of the mind to God"; and, in ecstasies of devotion, man is raised above all earthly cares and fears. The Jewish Mystics compare the action of prayer upon the human spirit to that of the flame on the coal. "As the flame clothes the black, sooty clod in a garment of fire, and releases the heat imprisoned therein, even so does prayer clothe a man in

JEWISH PRAYER

a garment of holiness, evoke the light and fire implanted within him by his Maker, illumine his whole being, and unite the Lower and the Higher Worlds" (Zohar).

This fine description of Jewish prayer is that of Dr. J. H. Hertz, the late Chief Rabbi of the British Empire, in the introduction to his commentary to the Prayer Book. Dr. Hertz favours the supernaturalistic interpretation of prayer. For him, prayer is an attempt by man to get into touch with Ultimate Being, with a Reality whose existence is independent of his own mind. As a devout and traditionally minded Jew, Hertz cannot accept those modern theories which, while not denying the efficacy of prayer, prefer to explain its value in purely natural terms. In a penetrating paper, delivered before the Rabbinical Assembly of America, Professor Abraham Joshua Heschel, critically examines these theories and reveals their inadequacies.

The first theory criticised by Heschel is that of "religious behaviourism," according to which the chief value of prayer lies in its effect in successfully continuing the Jewish tradition. The synagogue prayers are the best means of keeping the sense of tradition alive and of forging a link between this generation and past generations of Israel. But, as Heschel remarks, "Wise, important, essential, and pedagogically useful as the principle of 'respect for tradition' is, it is grotesque and self-defeating to make of it the supreme article of faith."

A kindred notion is that which sees prayer as the identification of the worshipper with the group to which he belongs, it is the means of making the Jew aware that he is part of the people of Israel. This doctrine of prayer as a social act sees God as the epitome of the ideals of the group. But this is to equate a political phenomenon with worship. It is true that a Jew never worships as an isolated individual but as a part of the people Israel, yet it is within the heart of every individual that prayer takes place.

Finally, there is what Heschel calls the "doctrine of religious solipsism," according to which prayer is a subtle form of auto-suggestion, it is addressed to "the good within ourselves." But is it really good for our psychic health to deny that God hearkens to prayer and yet pray "as if" He did because of the therapeutic effects of prayer? Is it not an old-fashioned and short-sighted psychology to assume that duplicity could be good for one's health? The real issue of prayer is not prayer; the issue of prayer is God. One cannot pray unless he has faith in his own ability to accost the infinite, merciful, eternal God.

This brief survey of Heschel's critique does not do justice to a most able exposition. The reader is advised to consult the original essay in the Proceedings of the Rabbinical Assembly of America, Vol. xvii, 1954. Here he will find, too, the opinion of a prominent member of the Reconstructionist school, Rabbi Eugene Kohn, who believes that it is not so absurd as Heschel thinks to pray to God conceived as a "cosmic process." We shall have occasion to refer to the points raised in this controversy in the chapter on Praising God. It is as well, however, to note that the rejection of the natural theories as inadequate in themselves does not, of course, rule them out as *supplementary* reasons for the value of prayer. Jewish prayer does provide the Jew with a powerful means of identifying himself with his people and with its past. And the idea of praying to the good in ourselves is not entirely unknown in the traditional Jewish sources. It appears to be mirrored in the remarkably bold rabbinic statement (for long the target of critics of the Talmud, insensitive to its quaint wisdom) that God Himself prays—His prayer being: "May it be My will that My mercy may suppress My anger, and that My mercy may prevail over My attributes, so that I may deal with My children in the attribute of mercy and, on their behalf, stop short of the limit of strict justice" (*Ber.* 7a).

Prayer as a Duty.

Is the duty to pray of Biblical origin? Undoubtedly there are many prayers in Scripture; most of the Biblical heroes pray; but is there a direct Biblical command that the Israelite should pray? The great Maimonides, in his Code of Jewish Law, answers in the affirmative, taking his stand on the rabbinic exegesis of a Biblical verse.

> *It is a positive precept to pray each day, as it is said: "And ye shall serve the Lord, your God. . . ." (Ex. xxiii, 25). Tradition teaches that the service spoken of here is prayer, as it is said: "And to serve Him with all your heart" (Deut. xi, 13). "What is service of the heart?" ask the Sages, "prayer!" But the number of the prayers and the form of prayers are not Biblical nor is a fixed time for prayer enjoined in the Bible (Yad, Tef. I, i).*

Other eminent, medieval authorities cannot see eye to eye with Maimonides on this question. For them there can be no *command* to pray for the essence of prayer is its spontaneity. There is much truth in the saying that the

WHAT IS JEWISH PRAYER?

Bible is God's gift to Israel, the Prayer Book is Israel's gift to God; though moderns would not wish to underestimate the human element in the Bible nor need we eliminate divine inspiration from the composition of the Prayer Book. In this connection a letter, written by Shneor Zalman of Ladi (1747-1812), the founder of the philosophical Habad movement in Hassidism, to a friend of the movement, is of interest.

> *For though the form of the prayers and the duty of praying three times a day is of rabbinic origin the idea of prayer and its essence is the foundation of the whole Torah. Namely, to know God, to recognise His greatness and His splendour with a serene and perfect mind and an understanding heart, that a man should concentrate on these thoughts until the rational soul is awakened to love God, to cleave to Him and to His Torah and to desire His precepts.*[1]

Types of Prayer.

There is more than one type of prayer. The earliest prayers were those of petition, in which God is entreated to grant man's request. There are, in addition, higher forms of prayer—the prayer of *thanksgiving* for favours received; the *penitential* prayer, asking God for forgiveness of sins; and the *doxology*, the prayer of praise.[2]

[1] Quoted by Teitelbaum in *Harav Miladi*, Warsaw, 1913, p. 213.
[2] An account of the different types of prayer is given in the article on Prayer in the *Universal Jewish Encyclopedia*, Vol. VIII, p. 617.

JEWISH PRAYER

Generally speaking, while simple faith finds no difficulty in the idea of prayer, various thinkers have been vigorous in their attacks on prayer, their wrath being directed especially against the prayer of petition. In the Jewish sources, we find the philosophers trying hard to reconcile prayers for life, for health, for food, sunshine and rain, for possessions and many children, with the idea of a universe governed by law, while the mystics tended to look upon such prayers as a form of egoism. For these latter the self must be transcended in prayer but petitionary prayers call attention to the ego and its desires. Consequently, both philosophers and mystics prefer to dwell on the spiritual effects of prayer and favour prayers of adoration and thanksgiving to those of petition. However, all the types of prayer are found in the Prayer Book. In the next chapter the suggestions that have been made to defend the validity of petitionary prayer will be noted.

The Regulation of Prayer.

There is bound to be some tension in the life of prayer between the idea of prayer as a spontaneous act, free from all conventional bonds, and the detailed rules and regulations that are inseparable from an established ritual of prayer. One of the counts registered against the Hassidim by their opponents was their neglect of the regulations governing the times of prayer. " The son can approach his father at any time of the day," argued the Hassidim, " if his father loves him and he loves his father." But Dr. Hertz has well said :

> *The regulations concerning the minutiæ of prayer are many: the opening treatise of the*

WHAT IS JEWISH PRAYER?

Talmud, Berachoth, is entirely devoted to the subject. Schürer and other Christian theologians contend that these regulations must have stifled the whole spirit of prayer. But this is a controversial fiction; as if discipline in an army, or laws in a country, necessarily suppressed patriotism. In fact, rule and discipline in worship increase *devotion: without them the noblest forms of adoration are unknown. The same is seen in the kindred realm of poetry. Elaborate schemes of metre and rhyme alone—witness the Greek poets, or Shelley, Goethe, Hugo—seem to render the highest poetry possible. With it all, none realised better than the rabbis the need for prayer to be true " service of the heart." He who prays must remember before Whom he stands, they said; and it was neither the length, nor the brevity, nor the language of the prayer that mattered, but the sincerity. " The All-merciful demands the heart," is their teaching.*

CHAPTER II

Does God Answer Prayer?

The Hebrew Prayer Book contains many petitions, most of them on behalf of the community rather than the individual worshipper, yet all assuming that God answers the prayers of those who pray to Him. Isaac Leeser writes:

> *God is not less omniscient because we are taught to pray to Him, nor is He less good because He awaits our humiliation before He grants us relief; but we must assure in general terms that the expression of our wants in prayer is one of the duties incumbent on us, in common with all others; a test whether we are obedient and thereby deserving the divine favours, or whether we are obdurate and therefore deserving the continuance of the evil which afflicts us, as a just recompense for our transgressing in not recognising the divine Power, in whose hand alone our enlargement is placed* (Quoted in the Jewish Encyclopedia, Vol. x, p. 169).

On the other hand, most people know from personal experience how often the hope for a better future is frustrated and how the prayers of even a good man often remain unanswered. The Psalmist's cry of confidence: "I have been young and now am old; yet I have not seen the righteous forsaken, nor his seed begging bread" (Psalm xxxvii, 25), is convincing evidence of the strength of his faith in a moment of poetic enthusiasm. It cannot have been meant as a statement of observable fact for as such its contradiction is met with at every turn. Good men do go hungry at times with their prayers unanswered. The kind of solution advanced by Leeser that prayer is a test of obedience, is too easy; the problem is far too complex to be casually dismissed in dogmatic fashion.

The problem belongs in part to the wider question—the most difficult question the religious person has been confronted with ever since men began to think about God—why do the righteous suffer? There is much speculation on this in Jewish sources but when all that can be said about it has been said the mystery remains. "If I knew Him I would be Him," wrote a medieval Jewish thinker. Only God Himself can know His plan and His purpose in full, only the Infinite can comprehend the Infinite. Man with his finite mind can obtain, at the most, only a glimpse of a tiny fragment of the truth. There is much in the observation that difficulties of this kind are inseparable from the conception of God that is Judaism's; man with his limited grasp is bound to find his understanding of God's ways partial and inadequate. A religion whose adherents were not called upon to face problems of this nature would certainly be false, for the God Who is both transcendent and immanent, Who, in the words of the Jewish mystics, "fills all worlds and surrounds all worlds," cannot be contained in the mind of man. Yet, the consideration of the following points may contribute to an understanding of why it is expecting the impossible to expect that God should always answer prayer.

The first consideration is that men often pray for things they believe to be of benefit to them which in reality are harmful. Every person who prays knows of examples of this; when God has been entreated to grant a desire, to fulfil a wish, and when there has been acute disappointment when the request has remained unanswered, only for the worshipper to have later discovered that it would not have been to his advantage for God to have acceded to his request. It is said that a little girl prayed repeatedly for a bicycle, without success. "You see, taunted her unbelieving friend, "God does not answer prayer." "Oh yes He does," answered the girl, "His answer was No!"

No! is also an answer. There is a legend told in the Talmud of a miracle-working saint, Haninah ben Dosa, whose prayers on behalf of others were frequently answered but who, in spite of the great poverty in which he lived, refused to pray for himself. One Sabbath eve there was no food in the house and, in her anxiety to honour the holy day in the accustomed manner with good food and drink, the wife of the saint implored him to pray for riches. Realising the justice of her plea, he entreated God to grant him wealth so that he would have greater opportunities of serving Him. Immediately, a hand reached down from heaven, holding a golden table leg which it gave to Haninah. That night he had a curious dream, in which he was escorted to Paradise, where he observed the righteous sitting at three-legged tables while he and his wife sat at a table with only two legs. On waking he told the dream to his wife, who urged him to pray that the golden leg be taken back. He did so and a hand reached once more from heaven and took the gift

DOES GOD ANSWER PRAYER?

back again. The legend concludes with the observation that it was a greater miracle for the gift to have been taken back than for it to have been given in the first place.

A quaint but profound comment on the problems of human life—for, according to the religious view, what a man makes of his life matters far more than the situation in which he finds himself. Here is a man who though in desperate need himself, though struggling constantly against bitter poverty, was able to pray for others and to inspire them with confidence and hope. Here is a man whose life was an eloquent testimony to the power of the human spirit and the indomitable human will. For such a man to have been blessed with wealth would have meant the *raison d'être* of his existence being taken from him. His prayer for the material goods of life had to remain unanswered if he was to find his true fulfilment. Of how many artists, thinkers, poets, and saints, who starved in the pursuit of beauty, truth, and goodness, who preferred to go in want rather than debase their God-given talents, was this true? Their heroic struggle against adversity was an essential part of their greatness. Their lives were noble precisely because of their demonstration that the human will can win beauty of ugliness, truth of error, triumph of degradation, victory of defeat, and glory of squalor. They were like Wordsworth's Happy Warrior:

> *Who, doomed to go in company with Pain*
> *And Fear and Bloodshed miserable train!*
> *Turns his necessity to glorious gain.*

For them, material success would have meant, in the words of the legend, that their table in heaven would have been unstable and incomplete.

The second consideration is that the interests of one

human being may conflict with those of other human beings so that for God to answer his prayer means that He must refuse to answer theirs. Where the raincoat manufacturer prays for rain and the farmer for fine weather the prayer of one of them must go unanswered. Each person is naturally concerned chiefly with his own needs, his own desires, his own hopes, but God is concerned with the needs of all men. The illustration has been given of a fly on a Rembrandt painting whose progress is impeded by a blob of paint. The fly cannot see any purpose in that blob of paint, it only knows that there is an obstacle to its progress. But the human being who observes the painting from a distance knows that without that particular blob of paint the picture would be incomplete. A man finds his hopes frustrated, he pushes against circumstances, he tries to escape from his burdens without success and God is silent to his entreaties. But man sees only a fragment of the truth. God alone sees it whole and He alone knows why those obstacles have to be there.

The analogy is, of course, far from perfect. For one thing, the blob of paint, while of value from the human point of view, has no purpose whatsoever from the point of view of the fly, whereas the belief in a benevolent Creator implies that He is concerned with the fate of each one of His creatures. Yet, inexact though it is, the illustration does afford some little help in enabling us to see that many of our difficulties about God's silence in the face of supplication are the result of our inevitably restricted vision and that if only we could observe God's plan at work in its entirety we would understand His silence.

Mature consideration of this very difficult problem brings one to the realisation that, while we are not, in the religious view, at the mercy of blind irrational forces, but the children of a benevolent Father, we cannot hope to see, as it were, God's plan at work. For what would happen if every time we prayed to God our prayers were answered, if every time a sick person turned to Him in prayer he was healed, every time a needy person cried to Him for help he became wealthy, every time a foolish man entreated Him for understanding he became wise? Then not only would synagogues be crowded to capacity but there would no longer be any merit in synagogue attendance. From an act of worship, a demonstration of faith, a desire for communion with God, synagogue attendance would degenerate into a system of incantation in which thaumaturgy had replaced devotion. The mystics express this idea by speaking of God hiding Himself that man may find Him, or, in other words, virtue must at times go unrewarded if man's freedom to choose the good is not to be taken from him.

The expressions in the liturgy that speak in terms of man pleading his cause before an undecided God, whom he seeks to influence, must not be taken too literally. God does not change His mind. " For He is not a man that He should repent" (I Sam. xv, 29). In the view of those who have given serious thought to this whole question of petitionary prayer, when men pray to God they ought to think in terms of coming nearer to Him; by bringing their requests to Him they ought to try to link their needs to His will. In this view, the man who entreats God is saying in so many words: " I ask this of God and by asking it of Him I acquire the proper attitude to the request."

This is one of the answers to the question why pray at all if God knows all our needs in advance. The philosopher, Joseph Albo (*c.* 1380-*c.* 1445), in the section of his famous *Book of the Principles of the Jewish Faith* which deals with prayer, thus states this problem:

> *The reason which leads men to doubt the efficacy of prayer is the same as that which leads them to deny God's knowledge. Their argument is as follows: Either God has determined that a given person shall receive a given benefit, or He has not so determined. If He has determined, there is no need of prayer; and if He has not determined, how can prayer avail to change God's will that He should now determine to benefit the person, when He had not so determined before? For God does not change from a state of willing to a state of not willing, or vice versa. For this reason they say that right conduct is of no avail for receiving a good from God. And similarly they say that prayer does not avail to enable one to receive a benefit, or to be saved from an evil which has been decreed against him* (Ikkarim iv, 18).

God does know all our needs but by bringing them to His Presence we elevate them and this in itself is an additional reason why they should be satisfied. To take the prayers for wealth and for knowledge, these are, in themselves, neutral things; they can be used for both good and evil ends. But by asking them of God, Who wants man to use them for good, the request serves as a reminder of God's will so that its whole complexion is changed.

The man of prayer, if he is wise, does not imagine that his prayers can influence his life without reference to natural causes. The man of prayer has no quarrel with the natural processes of cause and effect revealed by science; his only plea is that the existence of a new dimension be recognised.

> *The true claim of faith is mainly, as Professor Maritain contends, that humanism should recognise two dimensions—the vertical as well as the horizontal, the Godward as well as the manward relationship. And this claim should be regarded, not as a basis for a forced diplomatic compromise, a reluctant concordat between incompatible rival powers, but as something dictated by the nature of reality* (G. O. Griffith in "*Makers of Modern Thought,*" Lond., 1948, pp. 17-18).

Finally, the point has been made that for the saintly person his needs are his *excuse* for confronting God in prayer. Whether or no his requests are granted the opportunity to address his Maker is for him the supreme privilege, much as an affectionate son welcomes the opportunity of discussing his problems with his father irrespective of whether a solution to them all emerges from the discussion. A rare individual of this kind is not bothered by the problems raised in this chapter. With Meredith he says: " Who rises from prayer a better man, his prayer is answered."

In line with this thought, Rabbi J. L. Alter (1847-1905), the " Gerer Rebbi," in his commentary to Psalms, remarks:

> *Although it appears obvious that a man should pray when he is in need, but the truth is that the chief value of prayer is that the mind of the worshipper be on the prayer itself, not that the request be granted. For even when a man entreats God to grant his desire yet when he engages in*

> *prayer he should forget his needs and be affected solely by the praise of God. It may then happen that his request will be granted because it caused him to turn to God in prayer (Sefath Emeth, Psalm xviii, 7).*

The eighteenth-century Talmudist, Jacob Emden (1697-1776), expresses this thought even more emphatically in the introduction to his commentary to the prayer book (the Jacob Emden Prayer Book is one of the most popular Jewish books of devotion, used especially by the Hassidim in their worship). The following free translation conveys the basic idea, but for Emden's skilful use of Hebrew-rhymed prose the reader must consult the original.

> *However, it is essential that you know how to be careful when you make supplication for man's needs. God forbid that your intention should be for the gratification of your own desires, for this is self-worship, of which God has no desire, indeed it is abhorrent in His eyes. . . . Therefore, when a man asks of God his material needs, such as health, riches, peace, and other material perfections, his intention should be that these will help him to serve his Creator, seeing that a man cannot properly serve God if he lacks the material goods of life, which are God-given aids for the aim he really desires—the improvement of the soul.*

CHAPTER III

Praising God

Even a cursory inspection of the Jewish Prayer Book is sufficient to show the prominent place the prayer of adoration occupies in it. In obedience to the old rabbinic ruling, the Jew recites the praises of God before he petitions for his needs. Among the many doxologies in the prayer book, is the *Kaddish,* the great prayer of sanctification recited by mourners in the spirit of faith which refuses to allow death to have the final word.

If prayers of adoration are exempt from the criticism levelled against petitionary prayers, they are responsible for difficulties peculiar to them. Does God need our praises? He, Whose perfection is above all perfection, Who lacks nothing, what can it mean to Him that human beings declare how wonderful He is? Would we not tire of a man who persisted in flattering us? These and similar questions are often asked, and it cannot be denied that the failure to discover an adequate reply to them is the cause of much of the defection from the habit of prayer.

The trouble is that we think of God in human terms—this, indeed, is the only way we *can* think of Him. When Voltaire said that God created man in His image and man returned the compliment he was only stating the obvious that if we are to think about God at all we must describe Him in anthropomorphic terms. But unless we make the

JEWISH PRAYER

mental reservation that God cannot really be so described—cannot in fact be described at all—we are in danger of distorting our religious outlook. On a tombstone in an English village there was found this comically pathetic inscription, indicative of the way many people think of God:

> *Here lies Martin Elbingrod*
> *Have mercy on my soul, Lord God.*
> *As I would do were I Lord God,*
> *And you were Martin Elbingrod.*

And long ago Xenophanes remarked:

> *The Æthiopians say that their Gods are snub-nosed and black-skinned, and the Thracians that theirs are blue-eyed and red-haired. If only oxen and horses had hands and wanted to draw with their hands or to make the works of art that men make, then horses would draw the figures of their Gods like horses, and oxen like oxen, and would make their bodies on the model of their own.*[1]

Judaism has always sternly warned against the making of any image of God. Whenever the Talmudic sages hesitatingly attributed human qualities to God they called attention to the inadequacy of the description by the word *kebheyakhol*, " as if it were possible." The late Rabbi Kook, the first Chief Rabbi of Palestine, wisely said that the sceptic and the unbeliever fulfil a useful rôle from the religious point of view, for by their determined onslaught against the cruder notions of divinity commonly held, they compel religious people to re-examine

---

[1] Quoted by Arnold J. Toynbee in *A Study of History*, Lond., 1935, p. 1.

their ideas and arrive at a more refined and more spiritual conception.

This does not mean that the idea of a Personal God cannot be upheld. To speak of God as an impersonal Force or Principle is to deprive His would-be worshippers of the urge to worship. You cannot worship a cipher, said Chesterton. The God Jews worship is the God of Abraham, Isaac, and Jacob, Who hearkens to the prayers of His servants, Who can be addressed as " Our Father, our King," Who, in the words of William Temple, is more than personality, not less, Who is a *He*, not an *It*. A well-known twentieth-century scientist has said:

> *I am not much concerned whether I agree precisely with you in my conception or not, for both your conception and mine, must, in the nature of the case, be vague and indefinite. If you, in your conception, wish to identify God with nature you must perforce attribute to Him everything found in nature, such as consciousness and personality, or better,* super-consciousness *and* super-personality. *For you cannot possibly synthesise nature and leave out of it its most outstanding attributes —those which you know that you yourself possess. Nor can you get these* potentialities *out of nature no matter how far back you go in time. In other words, materialism as commonly understood is an altogether absurd and utterly irrational philosophy, and is indeed so regarded, I believe, by most thoughtful men.*[1]

Or as Professor Heschel puts it, in the essay noted above, as a comment on the rabbinic text, inscribed above the

[1] *The Autobiography of Robert A. Millikin*, Lond., 1951, p. 309.

ark in many synagogues: "Know before Whom you stand":

> Before Whom. *To have said before* what *would have contradicted the spirit of Jewish prayer. What is the most indefinite pronoun. In asking* what, *one is totally uncommitted, uninitiated, bare of any anticipation of an answer; any answer may be acceptable. But he who is totally uncommitted, who does not even have an inkling of the answer, has not learned the meaning of the ultimate question, and is not ready to engage in prayer. If God is a* what, *a power, the sum total of values, how could we pray to it? An " I " does not pray to an " it." Unless, therefore, God is at least as real as my own self; unless I am sure that God has at least as much life as I do, how could I pray.*[1]

Solomon Ibn Adret (1235-1310), the famous Spanish Talmudist, said all that can be said about this question of the God Who is hidden but Whom we address in prayer, when he pointed out that the usual form of benediction addresses God in both the second and third person, " Blessed art *Thou,* O Lord our God, King of the Universe, Who has sanctified us by *His* commandments. . . . " This is to convey the thought, remarks Adret, that though man can know God through His deeds, His essence cannot be known.

Thus, the idea of praising God has to be understood in a more refined sense than that God takes delight in His creatures telling Him how wonderful He is. Maimonides, the greatest Jew of the Middle Ages, goes so far as to teach that he who thinks of God in human terms has no

[1] *The Spirit of Jewish Prayer,* p. 162.

PRAISING GOD

share in the life to come. Abraham Ibn David, Maimonides' critic, refuses to follow him here, arguing that it is unreasonable to treat the Jew who entertains cruder notions of divinity as a heretic, for not everyone is capable of grasping the fact that the anthropomorphic Biblical and Rabbinic passages are not to be taken literally.[1] But, of course, in principle, Ibn David agrees with Maimonides that ideally only the more refined conception is permissible.

Maimonides quotes in this connection a well-known Talmudic anecdote. A certain person, reading the prayers in the presence of Rabbi Haninah, said, " God, the great, the valiant, the tremendous, the powerful, the strong, and the mighty." The Rabbi said to him: " Have you finished all the praises of your Master ? " And the parable is given of an earthly king, possessing millions of gold coin ; he was praised for owning millions of silver coin ; was this not really to dispraise him ? Now, notes Maimonides, the Rabbi does not say: " A king had millions of gold coin and he was praised as having hundreds " for this would imply that God's perfections though greater than those ascribed to men, are still of the same kind. The excellence of the simile " who possesses golden coins and is praised as having silver ones " is that this implies that human perfections cannot be applied at all to God. To Him they are defects.[2]

Why then praise God ? What is the purpose of such praise ? One of the reasons is that it is in this way that our minds are directed to higher ideals. By speaking of God as merciful, compassionate and just, man reminds himself that these qualities are worth making his own, that if he

[1] *Yad, Hil. Tesh.* III, 7.
[2] *Guide*, Part I, 59.

is to be God-like—and the imitation of God is the religious ideal—then he too must practise these virtues. The statement: " God is merciful " implies a belief that the universe is so constructed that compassion and kindliness and pity are absolute values and that for man to be in tune with life, at peace with the world and at peace with himself, he must cultivate these values. That the cruel and unfeeling and ungenerous person is a misfit out of tune with ultimate reality.

It goes deeper than this. God exists, but unless man recognises His existence and unless belief in His existence has some influence on man's life and character, then God does not exist for man. What is the meaning of the grand old Jewish doctrine of *Kiddush Hashem*, the Sanctification of God's Name, if not this, that God only exists for man when man recognises His sovereignty? The Sages had their own way of expressing this idea that, in a sense, God depends upon man, just as man depends upon God. In the Pesikta of Rab Kahana, an ancient rabbinic Midrash, we read: " Ye are my witnesses, the Eternal speaks, and I am God "; Rabbi Simeon ben Yohai said: " If ye give witness unto me, then I am the Eternal. If ye be not my witnesses, then I am not the Eternal, as it were."[1]

In a profound discussion of the difference between the acceptance of God's existence on philosophical grounds and His worship in religion, Dr. Leo Baeck wisely remarks:

> *The religion which man possesses rests therefore not simply on the fact that he recognises the existence of God. Rather do we find religion if we*

[1] See the fine article by Hugo Bergmann: " The Hallowing of the Name," in *Commentary*, March, 1952.

> *know that our life is bound up with something eternal, if we feel that we are linked with God, and that He is our God. He becomes our God if we, as the old phrase has it, love Him, if we get from Him our trust and humility, our courage and our peace, if we are able to raise ourselves up to Him and pray to Him, if we lay ourselves open in our innermost being to His revelation and law. The manner in which we grasp and express this inner connection is always only in the form of a similitude, and only an expression of the human soul. Our praising, and our talking about, God, with their use of "I" and "Thou," shape the features of the personal, and our meditating concerning God, which employs the word "He," forms the idea of Him. But whether we approach God with devout words of intimacy, or whether we wish to approach God by pure thought, whether the idea or the personal tries to express itself the more forcefully, is essentially the same, if only we make as our very own that on which all turns, that for us He is the One, that He is our God.*[1]

There is a need to worship in the human breast. This need finds its expression in the abasement of the savage before his totem pole, as well as in more refined types of worship. And unless this need is directed to the worship of the Supreme Being, the Source of all goodness, it will emerge in such obnoxious forms as the deification of the State and the apotheosis of the dictator, as the history of modern totalitarian movements has shown. In the year

[1] *The Essence of Judaism*, Lond., 1936, pp. 94-5.

1913, J. B. Bury published his *A History of Freedom of Thought,* in which religion is attacked in the name of freedom. It is not without significance that, in his epilogue to the 1952 edition, H. J. Blackham feels obliged to point out that much has happened since 1913. He notes that psychologists, who have been the deadliest critics of the objective truth of religious dogmas, have also been witnesses to the necessity of religion, and that the leader figure of the political religions is a substitute for the father whom most people cannot do without and whom the traditional religions provides in a time-honoured and much safer and more satisfactory way.

There is the final point that this urge to worship is in itself a validation of faith in God, our belief is a reasonable consequence to be drawn from the very fact of striving. A recent writer on religious psychology refers in this connection to a picturesque Arabic legend. A dervish was tempted by the devil to stop calling on Allah because Allah did not answer, " Here am I." An angel appeared to the dervish in a vision, with a message from Allah: " Was it not I who summoned thee to My service ? Did I not make thee busy with My name ? Thy calling ' God ' was my ' Here am I.' "

> *In that thou seekest thou hast the treasure found,*
> *Close with thy question is the answer found.*[1]

What has been said in this chapter on the need for a refined conception of the prayer of praise is not, of course, to disparage less sophisticated prayers or to deny

[1] From *The Individual and His Religion*, by Gordon W. Allport, Lond., 1951.

PRAISING GOD

that there can be something sublime in the simple faith of the man who praises God without being concerned about intellectual objections. Numerous are the sayings in the literature of Jewish piety that God loves the prayer of the unlearned uttered in the spirit of devotion. The following story from the Book of the Pious of Judah HeHasid (twelfth-thirteenth century) speaks for itself.

There was a certain man who was a herdsman, and he did not know how to pray. But it was his custom to say every day: "Lord of the World! It is apparent and known unto you, that if you had cattle and gave them to me to tend, though I take wages for tending from all others, from you I would take nothing, because I love you."

Once a learned man was going on his way and came upon the herdsman, who was praying thus. He said to him: "Fool, do not pray thus."

The herdsman asked him: "How should I pray?"

Thereupon the learned man taught him the benedictions in order, the recitation of the Shema and the prayer, so that henceforth he would not say what he was accustomed to say.

After the learned man had gone away, the herdsman forgot all that had been taught him, and did not pray. And he was even afraid to say what he had been accustomed to say, since the righteous man had told him not to.

But the learned man had a dream by night, and in it he heard a voice saying: "If you do not tell him to say what he was accustomed to say before you came to him, know that misfortune will overtake you, for you have robbed me of one who belongs to the world to come."

At once the learned man went to the herdsman and said to him: "What prayer are you making?"

The herdsman answered: " None, for I have forgotten what you taught me, and you forbade me to say: " If you had cattle."

Then the learned man told him what he had dreamed, and added: " Say what you used to say."

Behold, here is neither Torah nor works, but only this, that there was one who had it in his heart to do good, and he was rewarded for it, as if it were a great thing. For " the Merciful One desires the heart." Therefore, let men think good thoughts, and let these thoughts be turned to the Holy One, blessed be He.[1]

---

[1] From Nahum N. Glatzer's *In Time and Eternity*, Shocken Books, New York, 1946.

CHAPTER IV

Thanking God

Of the prayers of thanksgiving, the *berachah,* the benediction, usually beginning with the words: " Blessed art Thou, O Lord our God, King of the Universe," is the most common. The second-century teacher, R. Meir, said that the pious Jew should recite at least one hundred benedictions each day (*Men.* 43b). Maimonides divides the benedictions found in the prayer book into three groups. These are: the benediction for benefits received, *i.e.,* grace before and after meals, and the blessings on smelling fragrant woods and plants etc. ; the benedictions recited before the performance of religious duties ; and the expression of thanks for the wonders of nature, such as the blessings recited on observing lofty mountains or great deserts, on seeing a sage or a king and his court or on seeing the rainbow.

Apart from the benedictions to be recited by every Jew, a person who has some special reason for thanking God is expected to do so. We read in the Talmud that Rab Judah said in the name of Rab (third century): There are four classes of people who have to offer thanksgiving: those who have crossed the sea, those who have traversed the wilderness, one who has recovered from an illness, and a prisoner who has been set free (*Ber.* 5b). Following this, it is now the practice in the synagogue for one who has recovered from an illness, one who has travelled over the sea, whether by ship or by plane, and one who has been saved from a serious accident, to be called to the reading of the law, after which a special prayer of thanks is recited, its form being: " Blessed art Thou, O Lord our God, King of the Universe, who doest good unto the undeserving, and who hast also rendered all good unto me." To this the congregation responds: " He who hath rendered thee all good, may he do only good unto thee for ever " (*Singer's Prayer Book*, p. 148).

The objection to praising God noted in the previous chapter can be levelled too against the idea of thanking God. What can He gain from our thanks ? If, it is the essence of the Source of all goodness to benefit His creatures why should he require thanks for what He does ? Do we not think more highly of the person who gives charity without thought of repayment than of the donor who eagerly awaits the grateful thanks of the recipients of his bounty ? As in the case of praising God, the more satisfying interpretation here is that it is not so much that God requires thanks as that man needs to thank.

Thanking God has three chief advantages for man: it awakens in him a sense of gratitude and obligation, it reminds him to count his blessings, and it increases his appreciation of the good things of life.

First, the sense of gratitude and obligation. Judaism, it has often been remarked, teaches that life must be consecrated, not denied. There is nothing illicit in the enjoyment of material blessings but these should be looked upon as a divine trust, given that we may use it for good ends. This is one of the ideas behind such institutions as the Sabbath and the Sabbatical Year ; by refraining, at times, from the exercise of his control over nature, man is reminded that God and not he is nature's master. The illustration has been given in this connection of a thoroughfare, which the owner permits the public to use, but which he closes one day in the year to demonstrate that they use it by permission and not by right. Similarly, the benedictions recited before the enjoyment of life's blessings are the recognition that these are God-given. The third-century, talmudic teacher, Levi, famed for his interpretations of Biblical verses, solved the contradiction between the verse: *The earth is the Lord's and the fulness thereof* (Ps. xxiv, 1) and the verse: *The heavens are the heavens of the Lord, but the earth hath He given to the children of men!* (Ps. cxv, 16), by suggesting that the first verse speaks of earth's blessings before thanks have been given to God for them (*Ber.* 35 a-b).

The second advantage of thanking God is that it makes us aware of our good fortune, it helps to remind us of the many things we have to be thankful for, it enables us the better to come to grips with our environment and accept our status in life. In the words of the great teacher, Ben Zoma, in *Ethics of the Fathers*: " Who is rich ? He who rejoices in his portion " (*Ethics* iv, 1). Thanking God causes us to " rejoice in our portion."

This saying of Ben Zoma has often been misunderstood. It is not aimed against ambition as such. Provided that a man's aspirations are directed towards social aims, provided that, in his eagerness for a richer and better life, he does not use others as pawns in a selfish game of his own, a man's ambition can be innocent and may even be a force for good. Ben Zoma does not advise a man to be *satisfied* with his portion, but to *rejoice* in it—quite a different thing. He would hardly have subscribed to the sentiments expressed in the Victorian prayer of the menials:

> *God bless the squire and his relations,*
> *And keep us in our proper stations.*

There is a certain kind of restlessness, a divine discontent with present conditions and a longing to bring about a better state of affairs, without which all progress would be impossible.

What Ben Zoma does advise is the cultivation of the serenity of mind that enables a man to take the trials and tribulations of life in his stride, to face his disappointments and misfortunes philosophically and avoid feeling frustrated when the world does not give him what he imagines to be his due. This teaching was finely underlined by Jacob Anatoli (1194-1258), who, preaching the wisdom of contentment, said: " If a man cannot get what he wants, he ought to want what he can get."

Is this a counsel of perfection ? Is it really possible for a man so to attune himself to life that he can face all its vicissitudes with equanimity ? Ben Zoma speaks of a *portion,* that is, if a man believes that his life is a God-given portion, if he believes, with the sages, that a man cannot touch that which is destined for his neighbour, that man can find the blessing of tranquillity. The ideal Jew faces life's misfortunes, not as the stoic whose indifference to suffering is born of scepticism and black despair, nor as the man of little faith who becomes crushed under the burden of pain, but as the saint who exclaims: "Whatever God doeth is for the best." And one of the means to acquiring the wisdom of contentment is to thank God for the many blessings He has given to us.

Thirdly, the prayers of thanksgiving we recite produce

a heightened appreciation of life's worth. Hayyim Greenberg has forcibly expressed this view as follows:

> The words of the Midrash (I cannot for the moment recall the source) sound constantly in my ears: "The wicked is as one dead, even in his lifetime, for he sees the sun rise without reciting the blessing 'He Who formest light,' he sees its setting without reciting the blessing 'Who bringest on the evening twilight,' he eats and drinks without thanking God. But the righteous thank God for whatever they eat and drink and see and hear." What does the Midrash mean? Surely the mere recitation of "He Who formest light," and "Who bringest on the evening twilight" cannot infuse life into the righteous any more than the failure to recite them can deprive the wicked of life so that he should be "as one dead." The meaning of the Midrash is that the wicked is so dead spiritually that he cannot feel the need to recite the benediction and take delight in so doing; he is so dead that he cannot sense the mystery in the rising and setting of the sun, in the piece of bread that he eats and the measure of water he drinks; he is unaware of the eternal link between these things and the whole of existence and with God Who dwells in this existence. The wicked is as one dead because he has lost the sense of wonder, because he views the appearances of eternity as mundane happenings. He sees the externals of prayer without ever penetrating to the power hidden within it.[1]

[1] *Megilloth*, May, 1953, p. 66.

JEWISH PRAYER

The benediction, the prayer of thanksgiving, is then a means of re-awakening our sense of wonder at the miracle of life and the marvel of the mysterious universe we inhabit, a means of raising man from the mundane, the prosaic, and the commonplace into the realms of the ideal and the eternal. Greenberg effectively supports this theme with the quotation from Elizabeth Barrett Browning:

> *Earth's crammed with heaven,*
> *And every common bush afire with God;*
> *But only he who sees, takes off his shoes.*

CHAPTER V

The Use of Hebrew in Prayer

The question of Hebrew as the language of prayer has for long been a bone of contention between Jews of different theological schools. To put the case against the almost exclusive use of Hebrew as fairly as possible—why, it is frequently asked, should Jews whose mother tongue is English refrain from using this language when they pray ? Why should authority insist that their prayers be offered in what is to them an unfamiliar tongue, one which, with the best will in the world, they cannot understand ? Does not this insistence on Hebrew reduce the Synagogue prayers to an unintelligible gibberish without power to move or to inspire ?

It should be noted that, strange though this may seem, no question of *din*, of Jewish law, is here involved. The official code of Jewish law, the Shulchan Aruch, rules that prayers may be recited in any language (Shulchan Aruch, Orah Hayim, 101, 4). In a careful study of this question, Morris Joseph, in his *Judaism as Creed and Life*, while urging the retention of Hebrew for some of the prayers, especially those which proclaim the faith and hopes of Israel, favours the introduction of many more prayers in the vernacular on the grounds that the congregant should feel that he is no longer a mere spectator of rites which affect him only remotely and indirectly but a sharer in the Service. Joseph quotes the view of the devout author of the *Book of the Pious* (thirteenth century), who writes:

> *If one come to thee who doth not know Hebrew, and he is God-fearing and devout, direct him to pray in the language with which he is most familiar; for there can be no prayer unless the hearer understands, and if the heart knows not what the lips utter, what profit has a man of his worship?*

Yet, despite these considerations, those who opposed the use of prayers in the vernacular, insisting that Hebrew be retained, were not all hide-bound conservatives, opposed to change as such. Many of them had a deeper insight into the realities of the Jewish situation in the modern world and the spiritual needs of present-day Jewry, than the advocates of vernacular prayer.

There are a number of sound reasons for the retention of Hebrew, the first being the obvious one that the prayers were compiled in Hebrew and that a translation, however good, cannot capture the full flavour of the original. This is, of course, true of all good literature, where the precise manner in which the ideas are expressed contributes as much to its understanding and enjoyment as the ideas themselves. It is even true that an ancient classic loses much of its force if translated into modern speech in the same language, as St. John Ervine in his witty essay on the modernising of Shakespeare reminds us. Ervine takes as an extreme example Hamlet's famous soliloquy:

> *To be or not to be : that is the question :*
> *Whether 'tis nobler in the mind to suffer*
> *The slings and arrows of outrageous fortune,*

THE USE OF HEBREW IN PRAYER

*Or to take arms against a sea of troubles,
And by opposing end them?*

Render this into modern slang as: "For two pins I'd do myself in only I haven't the nerve" and the difference is at once seen. The meaning has not been radically altered but all the beauty of the original has been lost and only trite vulgarity remains.

It is more than a question of capturing the original meaning. Hebrew is a language rich in association. Its words and phrases have been used so long by Jews that they have acquired, as it were, a life of their own. The profoundest thoughts of the Jewish mind, the deepest longings of the Jewish heart, the most intimate glimpses into the Jewish soul, are revealed in the Hebrew language. The Jew who prays in Hebrew is using the tongue of the prophets and seers of Israel, he is clothing his thoughts in the identical words of Judaism's great classical writings. The English translation of *Torah* and *Mitzvah* as "Law" and "Precept," for example, utterly fails to convey the warmth and comprehensiveness of the original terms and it cannot succeed in evoking the Jewish emotional response.

Hebrew is *Leshon Hakodesh*, the sacred tongue. It has aptly been described as "the language of prayer"; there is more than a little truth in the saying of the old Scottish divine that one ought to learn Hebrew so as to be able to address the Almighty in His own language! The legend tells of Pharaoh who knew all the seventy languages but who, being ignorant of Hebrew, prevailed upon Joseph to teach him this language, without success. For a man may be an expert linguist, he may be a Semitic scholar of distinction and yet miss altogether the spiritual power of Hebrew. Into this language are woven the basic concepts of Israel's undying faith. A remarkable tribute to this aspect of Hebrew was paid by a prominent non-Jewish Hebraist, the author of one of the best Hebrew Grammars, in his introduction to that work:

> *When the principles underlying the language—which are simple enough—are understood, it is found to be characterised by an altogether extraordinary regularity. Hebrew is methodical almost to the point of being mechanical. The so-called irregular verbs, e.g., are, for the most part, strictly regular, springing no surprises, but abundantly intelligible to one who understands fundamental principles. It is therefore of the utmost importance that the learner be at pains to understand those principles . . . and if he goes forward to the study of the language with a faith in its regularity, he will find its very phonetic and grammatical principles* to be instinct with something of that sweet reasonableness, that sense of fair play, we might almost say that passion for justice, for which the Old Testament in the sphere of human life so persistently and eloquently pleads.

In a footnote, the author, J. B. Davidson, quotes the striking words of Deut. xvi, 20, " Justice, justice shalt thou pursue."

And what is true of the language of the Prayer Book is true of the Prayer Book itself. Theodor H. Gaster has finely said:

> *Throughout the ages, the Prayer Book has occupied a central position in Jewish life. More*

*than a mere manual of devotion, it is—in a sense
—Israel's personal diary, catching, as in a series
of exquisite vignettes, the scenes and moments
of her entire life, and recording, in a diversity of
moods and styles, her deepest and most intimate
emotions. Here, for those who have eyes and ears,
is Sinai on the one hand, and Belsen on the other;
the gleaming courts of the Temple, and the peeling
walls of a Polish klaus; the blare of the silver
trumpets, and the singsong of the Talmud
student; the colonnaded walks of a Spanish
town, and the narrow, winding lanes of Safed.
Here is a Gabirol effortlessly bringing down the
immortal to earth, and a Rhineland cantor
scribbling his earthiness into immortality. Here
is Luria panting desperately after the Celestial
Chariot, and Kalir pinning the glories of God to
an acrostic.*[1]

It is to history that we must go for a further reason for the retention of Hebrew. In the year 1845, a rabbinical conference was held in Frankfort to consider the question of changes in Jewish practice. This conference, dominated by the Reform party, voted that Hebrew was not essential to divine worship, whereupon Zecharias Frankel, the founder of the historical school in Judaism, withdrew from the conference. The majority of the rabbis present failed to understand why Frankel, who was by no means unaware of the need for changes, should be so concerned about what was, in their eyes, a minor adjustment, affecting no fundamental principle of the Jewish faith. Abraham Geiger alone understood

[1] "Modernising the Jewish Prayer Book," by Theodor H. Gaster, in *Commentary,* April, 1954.

Frankel's position, even though he disagreed with it. Geiger argued that language is a *national* matter and Judaism is a *religion* ; it was wrong to attempt to tie down religious expression to any one language. In other words, early Reform opposition to the use of Hebrew in public prayer was a necessary corollary of its anti-nationalistic interpretation of Judaism. According to Classical Reform theory, the Jews were not a nation ; they were Germans or Frenchmen or Englishmen or Americans of the Mosaic persuasion, no different, except for their religious beliefs, from Catholic or Protestant Germans, Frenchmen, Englishmen, and Americans.

Judaism, in this view, is a set of religious affirmations and practices binding on the Jew but the particularistic aspect of historic Judaism, which thinks of the Jews as a nation, was outmoded. The ancient Messianic hope should be reinterpreted as referring to the spread of the Jewish ideal in Western Society rather than in terms of a national restoration of the Jewish people in its ancient homeland. It was this conception of Judaism that Frankel was obliged to reject.

The subsequent events of Jewish history—the rise of antisemitism, the destruction of a third of the Jewish people, the emergence of the State of Israel—have caused Frankel's views to be shared by the majority of Jews. It is only right to mention that many Reform teachers have recognised that the Classical Reform position was a travesty of Jewish history and experience and have embarked on a complete re-thinking of their position in the light of the present-day situation. Most Jews today want to demonstrate the solidarity of the Jewish people and how better do this than by praying in Hebrew ? Only the spiritually insensitive can fail to

THE USE OF HEBREW IN PRAYER

be moved by the grandeur of the idea of Jews in America, in Israel, in Africa, in every part of the world, divided though they might be on many issues, unlike in many things, yet worshipping the same God and using the same language in that worship. " Thou art One, and Thy Name is One, and who is like unto Thy people Israel, one nation upon earth."

There is the further point that vernacular prayers, especially extemporaneous ones, do not only lack warmth and colour and soon become monotonous but they are almost always accompanied by an atmosphere of sanctimoniousness. Zangwill's description of the uncouth prayers in the little conventicle of the Sons of the Covenant, with its subtle blend of condescending pity and sympathy, yet manages, brilliantly, to convey the warmth of the traditional service.

> *They prayed metaphysics, acrostics, angelology, Cabbalah, history, exegetics, Talmudical controversies, menus, recipes, priestly prescriptions, the canonical books, psalms, love-poems, an undigested hotch-potch of exalted and questionable sentiments, of communal and egoistic aspirations of the highest order. It was a wonderful liturgy, as grotesque as it was beautiful; like an old cathedral, in all styles of architecture, stored with shabby antiquities and side-shows, and overgrown with moss and lichen—a heterogeneous blend of historical strata of all periods, in which gems of poetry and pathos and spiritual fervour glittered, and pitiful records of ancient persecutions lay petrified. And the method of praying these things was equally complex and uncouth, equally the bond-slave of tradition; here a rising*

and there a bow, now three steps backwards and now a beating of the breast, this bit for the congregation and that for the minister; variants of a page, a word, a syllable, even a vowel, ready for every possible contingency. Their religious consciousness was largely a musical box: the thrill of the ram's horn, the cadenza of a psalmic phrase, the jubilance of a festival "Amen" and the sobriety of a workaday "Amen," the Passover melodies, and the Pentecost, the minor keys of Atonement and the hilarious rhapsodies of Rejoicing, the plain chant of the Law and the more ornate intonation of the Prophets—all this was known and loved, and was far more important than the meaning of it all, or its relation to their real lives; for page upon page was gabbled off at rates that could not be excelled by automata. But if they did not always know what they were saying, they always meant it. If the service had been more intelligible, it would have been less emotional and edifying. There was not a sentiment, however incomprehensible, for which they were not ready to die or to damn (Children of the Ghetto).

Whatever else this is it is not moribund or dull and the modern Synagogue has preserved its freshness and vitality in so far as it has retained some of these modes, even while it has rightly rejected the more grotesque.

In the "days of faith," when the prayers were compiled, they were, of course, contemporaneous; the earlier prayers, at least, were expressed in language that people used in their daily lives. But there is much to be said for the view that in our more unimpressionable age prayer requires a more "remote" a more "traditional" language, if it is to avoid both the familiarity of the curate, who began his extemporaneous prayer with: "Dear God, you have read in this morning's newspaper, . . ." and the monotony that is inseparable from the frequent repetition of words in common use. As Robert Gordis says:

> While prayers in the vernacular were urged on the grounds that they added greater meaningfulness to the service, in practice they created a new and unexpected complication. Hebrew prayers chanted in the traditional manner could be repeated at almost every occasion without producing a sense of monotony in the worshipper. In the first instance, the traditional congregant was an active participant in the ritual instead of being a member of a silent audience. The mass chanting and swaying might not be very decorous by Western standards. It had the virtue, however, of being alive. The old psychological principle of "no impression without expression" embodied in Jewish prayer made the experience emotionally vibrant and satisfying. Second, the characteristic musical modes and Scriptural cantillations, which differ with the varying occasions of the year, served to create a distinct mood appropriate to the day and added variety and interest, even when the text remained the same.[1]

It has more than once been convincingly demonstrated that those Jewish communities in the past who, for one

---

[1] "A Jewish Prayer Book for the Modern Age," reprinted from *Conservative Judaism*, Vol. II, No. 1, October, 1945, p. 4.

reason or another, neglected Hebrew, even though they possessed prolific writers and thinkers on Jewish themes in other languages, doomed themselves to extinction and eventually vanished entirely from the Jewish scene without leaving any lasting impression. Two thousand years ago, there existed a flourishing Jewish community of over two million souls in Alexandria. In an amusing talmudic account of the size of the great basilica, used for prayer, it is said that this was so large that a special functionary was obliged to stand near the reader with a flag in his hand, which he would wave when the reader came to the end of a benediction, so that those near the door would know when to answer Amen ! The prayers in that and in the other Alexandrian synagogues were recited in Greek ; even the sacred scrolls were written, not in Hebrew, but in Greek. The result of this was that Alexandrian Jewish thought had hardly any direct influence on the subsequent development of Judaism. Its greatest thinker, Philo, was unknown to the mainstream of Jewish tradition. There is no definite reference to him in the talmudic literature: the first Jewish writer to mention him by name was Azariah de Rossi, the Italian Jewish humanist, writing as late as the sixteenth century.

This lead to perhaps the most important consideration of all, the pedagogic value of Hebrew as the language of prayer. It must be admitted that many people are making a real sacrifice when they pray in Hebrew. Every Jewish minister in English-speaking lands knows devout people who would derive far more from the synagogue service if more English was used in the service. Yet a Jewish saint once said that the Jewish expression for self-sacrifice, *mesirath nephesh*, can mean " offering up the *soul*," that is, at times *spiritual* as well as material, sacrifices have to

THE USE OF HEBREW IN PRAYER

be brought in the defence of faith. And the sacrifice involved in the retention of Hebrew is a worthwhile one for it is precisely this insistence on Hebrew that provides a tremendous impetus for its study. It is the use of Hebrew in prayer, the traditional Bar Mitzvah ceremony, conducted in Hebrew, which encourage parents who are at all interested in the Jewish education of their children to have them introduced to the study of the language at an early age. At this late hour, when Hebrew is once again a living language and when there is renewed interest in it everywhere, it would surely be a retrograde step to use any other language in the service of the synagogue. The knowledge of the Hebrew language unlocks the doors of the Jewish spiritual treasure-house. As has been said of Greek in a somewhat different sense, the knowledge of Hebrew provides the key to Paradise.

CHAPTER VI

The Technique of Prayer

The talmudic rabbis attached a great deal of importance to *Kavvanah* in prayer. *Kavvanah*, from a Hebrew root meaning "to direct," is the direction of the mind to God, the act of concentration on the meaning of the prayers and the awareness that the worshipper confronts God and is confronted by Him when he prays. Those ancient Jewish teachers were sufficiently realistic to recognise that the art of concentration in prayer is not easily mastered and they accordingly ruled, and their ruling was followed by the later Codes, that it is not necessary to repeat prayers recited without *Kavvanah*, provided that the first verse of the *Shema* (the Jewish declaration of faith) and the first benediction of the *Amidah* (the silent prayer, recited while the worshipper stands) were recited with *Kavvanah*. But this was a minimum demand. The ideal was that of proper concentration during all the prayers; that, in the words of the rabbis in a similar situation, "the heart and lips should egree," "*piv velibo shavvim.*"

> *In prayer the lips ne'er act the winning part,*
> *Without the sweet concurrence of the heart.*
> (Herrick.)

> *When wood burns it is the smoke alone that rises upwards, leaving the grosser elements below. So*

THE TECHNIQUE OF PRAYER

it is with prayer. The intention (Kavvanah) *alone ascends to heaven.* (Besht)

"Prayer without *Kavvanah*," the old saying has it, "is like a body without the soul." "We must bear in mind," writes Maimonides, in his *Guide for the Perplexed*,[1] "that all such religious acts as reading the Law, praying, and the performance of other precepts, serve exclusively as the means of causing us to occupy and fill our minds with the precepts of God, and free it from worldly business; for we are thus, as it were, in communication with God, and undisturbed by any other thing. If we, however, pray with the motion of our lips, and our face toward the wall, but at the same time think of our business; if we read the Law with our tongue, whilst our heart is occupied with the building of our house, and we do not think of what we are reading; if we perform the commandments only with our limbs, we are like those who are engaged in digging in the ground, or hewing wood in the forest, without reflecting on the nature of those acts, or by whom they are commanded, or what is their object. We must not imagine that in this way we attain the highest perfection: on the contrary, we are then like those in reference to whom Scripture says, 'Thou art near in their mouth, and far from their reins'" (Jer. xii, 2).

One of the best-known rabbinic works on Judaism is Isaiah Horovitz's (b. Prague *c*. 1555; d. Safed *c*. 1628) *Shene Luhoth Haberith* (generally abbreviated to *Shelah*), "The Two Tablets of Stone." In this work, in the section dealing with prayer, the author quotes from an earlier work a number of aids to devotion. Few would

[1] iii, 51.

deny that for the contemplative virtues it is to men like Horovitz that we must go, men who had the time, the patience and the inclination to engage in spiritual exercises in a manner beyond the reach of most men in our more hectic age.

The first aid to concentration that Horovitz speaks of he calls *Torah*. If, he says, a man devotes some of his time to the study of the Torah, if he gives some thought to his faith, if he practises his Judaism in his daily life, he will be better equipped for the life of prayer than the man who comes to his prayers from a world in which spiritual values are remote. In this connection the verse in Deut. xxxii, 47 is quoted: "For it is no vain thing for you," upon which the Rabbis comment, "If it is a vain thing, *i.e.*, if you can see no value in the Torah, then it is you who are to blame." Or, as someone once said, synagogues are only empty if people are empty!

It is paradoxical but true that only those Jews really appreciate the value of the synagogue and of prayer for whom Judaism is far more than the synagogue and prayer. It is recorded in the Talmud that when a Babylonian Rabbi saw that his friend was taking too long over his prayers he accused him of "neglecting eternal life and engaging in temporal life," because the time spent in long, drawn out prayer could have been far better employed in the study of the Torah. This is not to minimise the value of prayer but a reminder that, in the name of prayer itself, the faith of the Jew must be co-extensive with life itself if it is to have an effect on his devotional life. Horovitz would certainly have subscribed to the saying that important though it is to build synagogues for Jews it is even more important to build Jews for the synagogue.

THE TECHNIQUE OF PRAYER

A prominent American Jewish layman, a fine Jewish scholar and writer, said this to a conference of Rabbis some years ago:

I am not angry at a Jew who does not attend synagogue. I am not angry at a Jew who does not pray. I want to know why doesn't he go to synagogue; why doesn't he pray? If it's merely a humra *(a special act of piety), then I don't want to pray. But if going to the synagogue is not a* humra, *but it is joy of life and if prayer enriches me then without your reminding me I'll go to synagogue, I'll pray.*

We are confronted here not merely with the problem of desertion. It's not desertion. A Jew, or any other human being for that fact, who does not know what it means to have an hour of solitude, who doesn't know what to do with himself when he remains alone for an hour or two; if he has nothing to say to himself, only to others; if he hasn't developed the gift of contemplation—what makes you ask that Jew to be a professing, courageous Jew when he is empty, when he has no capacity for experiencing things?

It's a therapeutic question, and, from that point of view, I don't recognise a rabbi if he is not a healer, if he cannot perform a therapeutic and educational task.

The question is not about asking Jews back to synagogue. There is something preceding, something prior to that question—how to awaken in that Jew the sense of values which he has lost, and, when the sense of values has already been reawakened in him, how to link up that sense of

JEWISH PRAYER

> *spiritual values with Judaism, with the specific values of Judaism.*[1]

Horovitz's second aid he calls *hiddush*, "renewal." The reference is to the need for avoiding monotony in prayer by bringing variety and freshness to the services. A talmudic ruling is followed here, in which it is stated that if a man wants to offer after an additional prayer, after he has recited the statutory ones, he may only do so if he is able to introduce some fresh petition, otherwise his voluntary offering is mere mechanical repetition. What Horovitz suggests is that every time prayer is offered, an attempt should be made to link it with some current event in the life of the worshipper. In the prayer for health, for example, the mind should be directed towards a sick person one knows, in the prayer for peace the mind should dwell on the present difficult world situation, and so on. Thus, the element of topicality would make the prayers more vital so that it would be easier to concentrate.

This leads him to the third aid—*Tzorech*, "need." The man who is in need, he who has drunk deeply of the cup of suffering, finds no difficulty in concentrating when he entreats his Maker to remove his pain. The Psalms, the most exquisite gems in the world's devotional literature, were all composed by men whose needs were great; witness the number of times such words as "the poor," "the afflicted," "the needy," occur. The Psalmists pray to God out of the straits or out of the depths.

> *The Psalmist says:* "*Out of the depths I cry unto thee, O Lord.*" *What relation is there between*

[1] Hayyim Greenberg in an address delivered at the forty-sixth annual convention of the Rabbinical Assembly of America, Proceedings, Vol. X, 1947, p. 274.

THE TECHNIQUE OF PRAYER

" the depths " and " Lord " ? When there is neither depths, nor horror, nor despair, man does not see God and does not call to Him. (Lev Shestov)

Most people have needs and ought to find no difficulty in concentrating on them when bringing them before God. But what, continues Horovitz, of the rare individual who feels that he lacks nothing ? Let him consider his spiritual needs, replies the author. Let him pray for wisdom, for nobility of character, for the strength of will to conquer his failing. Let him pray for those less fortunate than he. Let him pray for God to remove suffering from Israel and from all mankind. Pious Jews of old even rose to the spiritual heights of prayer on behalf of God Himself, as it were. Of praying, as they called it, that the " Exile of the Shechina (the Divine Presence) " be brought to an end ; that the Presence should once again rest on the Holy Land and that all men be brought nearer to His service. Schechter once said that hostile critics may do their worst in belittling Israel's contribution to religion, this is something they cannot explain. The picture of a Jew of the old school, often in dire need himself, yet rising at midnight to pray for the exile of the Shechina to cease.

The next point Horovitz deals with is the use of Hebrew in prayer. He frankly confesses that it is far more difficult to concentrate when praying in Hebrew than when offering prayers in a more familiar tongue. Seeing that we do not think in Hebrew, a constant effort of the will in concentration is required when prayers are offered in this language. The author refers to the practice in his day of reciting some of the lamentations on the fast of Ab in Yiddish, the vernacular of sixteenth-century Jews in Poland, and how much easier it is to concentrate when these are being recited. However, his solution is not that Hebrew be discarded as the language of prayer. The weighty reasons for its retention have been noted above. What he does advise is that, if it is at all possible, Hebrew should be used by Jews in their daily conversations so that it becomes habitual for them to think in Hebrew. A mere pious hope this in those days but increasingly possible of realisation, nowadays, when Hebrew is a modern language and has become sufficiently flexible to express all the familiar thoughts and ideas. The acquisition by Jews of Hebrew as a second language provides them not only with a valuable link with the State of Israel but serves as a tremendous aid to concentration in prayer.

Some of the other points the author refers to have to do with decorum in the synagogue and the cultivation of the proper devotional atmosphere. Where these are present, concentration is easier; where they are absent, it becomes exceedingly difficult. Unlike many of the Polish Rabbis of his day, Horovitz does not approve of the practice of shaking at prayer, considering this a distraction. Nor does he approve of vociferous prayer; a gentle, almost inaudible tone is a definite aid to concentration. Following the ancient Rabbis, he quotes the verse describing Hannah's prayer as his authority for the meditative value of quiet prayer : " Now Hannah, she spoke in her heart; only her lips moved, but her voice could not be heard . . ." (I Sam. i, 13). It follows that Horovitz, and all the great masters of the art of prayer, would strongly have disapproved of the habit of engaging in conversation while the prayers are being read, the old argument that the synagogue is the *house* of God and the Jew feels " at home " there, notwithstanding.

THE TECHNIQUE OF PRAYER

The two final points made by Horovitz have to do with preparation for prayer and that the worshipper should allow himself ample time in which to pray. First, preparation. The ancients knew the secret of prayer because they understood the value of preparation. The Mishna is the first great Code of Jewish law, compiled by Rabbi Judah, the Prince, about the year two hundred of the common era. This work is more than a code of law in the narrow sense; it contains teachings about almost every aspect of Jewish life. Teachings given in the Mishnah, the standard authority for Jews, have additional importance in Jewish eyes. Consequently, seeing that the need for preparation in prayer is enjoined in the Mishnah, this was looked upon as essential. The Mishnah, in its first tractate, has this to say:

> *None may stand up to say the* Tefillah *(i.e., the statutory prayer, the* Amidah*) save in sober mood. The pious men of old used to wait an hour before they said the* Tefillah, *that they might direct their heart toward God. (Ber. v. 1)*

As a supplement to the Mishnaic teaching, the Talmud quotes this contemporaneous source:

> *Our Rabbis taught: One should not stand up to say the* Tefillah *while immersed in sorrow, or idleness, or laughter, or frivolity, or chatter, or idle talk, but only while rejoicing in the performance of some religious act. (Ber. 31a)*

"A modern American poet has described his art as one in which you prepare yourself for a poem to happen, in which you expose yourself to inspiration, while having made sure beforehand to acquire the techniques for making the most of the inspiration when it comes. This is true of the art of prayer" (Robert Langbaum). Louis I. Newman, in his Hassidic Anthology, tells of a man who was not a Hassid but who desired to witness for himself the behaviour of the Apter Rabbi, who had a great reputation as a man of prayer. The man visited the Apter synagogue, and found the Rabbi buried in thought and smoking his pipe. He dared not interrupt the Rabbi, but recited the morning prayers to himself, and then took a book and studied in it for some time. When noon came and the Rabbi made no movement to begin his Morning Prayers, the visitor whispered to him: "Rabbi, the time for the Morning Prayers is past." The Apter replied: "A man like you is satisfied to enter the synagogue and to commence his worship immediately. As for myself, it is different. I began the order of prayers earlier than you with the words: 'I give thanks before Thee' (the first words the devout Jew says on rising), and I began to think: 'Who am I to give thanks before the Lord?' I am still thinking of the same matter."

Finally, there is what Horovitz calls "time," the need for freedom during prayer from the tyranny of time, the ability to forget worldly preoccupations in the synagogue, the attempt to inhabit, albeit for a short space of time, a world in which the eternal matters more than the transient. There can be no real concentration in prayer with one eye on the clock. One of the most precious things the synagogue can give to the Jew is an opportunity for assessing the value of the life he leads, a breathing space to recollect his thoughts, a means of rediscovering his potentialities for good, amid the hurry and stress of what has become normal existence for twentieth-century man.

Horovitz concludes with a very human touch. There

THE TECHNIQUE OF PRAYER

are two kinds of people, he remarks, the *mithkavnim*, those who concentrate in prayer, and the *mithnahagim*, those for whom synagogue attendance is a mere pious habit. The latter are in the majority and the author, in his humility, prays that he should not belong to this group, though he very much fears that he does. Which sensible observation will be re-echoed by anyone who has ever striven to master the technique of prayer. One of the great Jewish saints observed that the most important prayer is the prayer to be taught how to pray!

CHAPTER VII

Congregational Prayer and the Synagogue

"Why bother to come to the synagogue for prayer? If I want to I can pray just as well at home!" This is no new question. The talmudic rabbis faced it squarely over fifteen hundred years ago. There is a remarkable passage in the Talmud (Ber. 6a) in which it is said that if ten people (a *minyan*, the quorum for congregational prayer) pray together the Divine Presence is with them. But, continues the Talmud, even if one man sits and studies the Torah the Divince Presence is with him. And the obvious question is asked—if the Divine Presence is with less than ten what is the significance of ten, why all the insistence in Jewish tradition on a *minyan*? If a man can commune with his Maker in solitude why should he worship together with others? The answer contains the whole philosophy of congregational worship. "To a gathering of ten," say the Rabbis, "the Divine Presence comes first; to less than ten it does not come till afterwards."

In other words, while it is possible for a man to pray anywhere, while God can be worshipped outside the synagogue, it is much more difficult if the atmosphere of devotion has to be created by a man's unaided efforts, if he is unable to draw on the spiritual power provided by the living example of his fellows. On his own a man has to be in the mood for prayer; he has to struggle to get in tune with the Infinite amid the many distractions of modern life. In the words of the Talmud, the Divine Presence comes to him afterwards, after the kind of preparation that is beyond the spiritual means of most people today, unless it be in exceptional circumstances, such as when a man is in trouble or in need. But in the synagogue, in which generations of Jews have poured out their hearts in worship and in which many likeminded people pray, the atmosphere is there. The religious emotions cannot fail to be stirred by the beauty of the music and the edifice, by the warmth and fervour of the worshippers, and, above all, by the feeling that the worshipper is not alone. As Friedrich Heiler[1] puts it:

> *The prayer of the congregation is meant to lift the individual to a higher stage of devotion. Narrow self-seeking wishes should be silenced in the presence of the congregation. The little and the weak who come to the meeting with low and earthly thoughts, should be carried to heights of religious yearning, should pray as the strong and creative pray; those who do not know what true prayer is, should here learn to pray and practise the art.*

Phillip Brooks says much the same thing:

> *A multitude of people gathered for a special purpose and absorbed for the time into a common interest has a new character which is not in any of the individuals which compose it. If you are*

[1] *Prayer* (translated by Samuel McComb, D.D.), Oxford University Press, 1932, p. 306.

JEWISH PRAYER

> *a speaker addressing a crowd you feel that. You say things to them without hesitation that would seem either too bold or too simple to say to any man among them if you talked with him face to face. If you are a spectator and watch a crowd while someone else is speaking to it, you can feel the same thing. You can see emotions run through the mass that no man there would have deigned to show or submitted to feel if he could have helped it. . . . Canning used to say that the House of Commons as a body had better taste than the man of the best taste in it, and Macaulay was much inclined to think that Canning was right.*[1]

As usual, the talmudic rabbis had their own effective way of expressing it. In the words of the Talmud quoted above, where a congregation gathers in prayer, the Divine Presence is there first.

Human beings have always looked upon large gatherings of people as a means of paying homage to a person or an idea. An empty synagogue is depressing because it implies that only the few congregants assembled are interested in prayer. A crowded synagogue, on the other hand, implies that Judaism is precious in the eyes of many people who assemble to participate in the expression of loyalty to its ideals. This idea, that the more people who participate in an act of worship, the more dignified that act becomes, was elevated by the Rabbis into an important principle, supported by the Biblical verse: " In the multitude of the people is the King's glory " (Proverbs, xiv, 28). This is the reason given in the Talmud for the ruling that the *Shofar* should be blown

---

[1] *Lectures on Preaching*, Lond., 1904, pp. 183-4.

on *Rosh Hashanah* during the second part of the service, when more people are likely to be present. For the same reason it was forbidden to sell a synagogue from a larger to a smaller town.

It remains, of course, true that private prayer has great value. Indeed, the evidence supports the view that congregational prayer as we know it today was a post-Biblical development and that the prayers found in the Bible are chiefly individual ones. Heschel, in the essay referred to earlier, writes:

> *It is true that a Jew never worships as an isolated individual but as a part of the people Israel. Yet it is within the heart of every individual that prayer takes place. It is a personal duty, and an intimate act which cannot be delegated to either the cantor or to the whole community. We pray with all Israel, and everyone of us by himself. Contrary to sociological theories, individual prayer came first, while collective prayer is a late phenomenon which is not even mentioned in the Bible.*

Yet the Rabbis were so convinced of the heightened significance of synagogal prayer that they praised it in the most elaborate terms. The following are some typical rabbinic comments on this subject:

> *Abba Benjamin said: a man's prayer is heard only in the synagogue (Ber. 6a). Rabin, son of R. Adda in the name of R. Isaac said: If a man is accustomed to attend synagogue and one day he does not go, the Holy One, blessed be He, makes inquiry about him (Ber. 6b). R. Helbo, in the name of R. Huna, says: Whosoever has a fixed place for*

his prayer has the God of Abraham as his helper. And when he dies, people will say of him: The pious man is no more, the humble man is no more, one of the disciples of our father Abraham! R. Helbo, in the name of R. Huna, says further: When a man leaves the synagogue, he should not take large steps. Abaye says: This is only when one goes from the synagogue, but when one goes to the synagogue, it is a pious deed to run. For it is said: Let us run to know the Lord *(Hosea vi, 3). (Ber. 6b.)*

R. Isaac said to R. Nahman: Why does the master not come to the synagogue to pray? He said to him: I cannot. He asked him: Let the master gather ten people and pray with them? He answered: It is too much trouble for me. Let the master ask the messenger of the congregation to inform him of the time when the congregation prays? He answered: Why all this? He said to him: For R. Johanan said in the name of R. Simeon b. Yohai: What is the meaning of the verse: But as for me, let my prayer be made unto Thee, O Lord, in an acceptable time *(Psalm lxix, 14). When is the time acceptable? When the congregation prays (Ber. 7b-8a).*

It is unnecessary to dwell at length on the importance of the synagogue in Judaism or of the influence of the synagogue on Christian and Moslem worship. " The synagogue represents something without precedent in antiquity; and its establishment forms one of the most important landmarks in the history of religion. It meant the introduction of a mode of public worship conducted in a manner hitherto quite unknown, but destined to become the worship of civilised humanity" (J. H. Hertz). The oldest extant account of a synagogue service is given by Philo:

> In fact they do constantly assemble together, and they sit down with one another, the multitude in general in silence, except when it is customary to say any words of good omen, by way of assent to what is being read. And then some priest who is present, or some one of the elders, reads the sacred laws to them, and interprets each of them separately till eventide; and then when separate they depart, having gained some skill in the sacred laws, and having made great advances toward piety.[1]

Wherever Jews wandered their first concern was to build a synagogue. According to the Zohar, the command to build a sanctuary includes the duty of erecting a synagogue. A scholar, says the Talmud, must not reside in a town in which there is no synagogue. Among the many details found in the early sources concerning the construction of the synagogue are that it must be higher than the other buildings of the town; that it should stand in the highest part of the town; that it should contain an ark and a raised platform, from which the law is read; and that it should have windows, so that the worshippers can see the heavens, or, according to some commentators, so that the light can enter. Apart from such details, great freedom is left to the architect. "There is no fixed form of synagogue architecture," remarks the famous eighteenth-century rabbinic authority, R. Ezekiel Landau, in a Responsum.

[1] C. D. Yonge: *The Works of Philo Judæus*, iv, p. 217f., quoted by Salo Baron in *The Jewish Community*, Vol. I, p. 89.

JEWISH PRAYER

The Rabbis insisted on decorous behaviour in the synagogue. "Synagogues must not be treated disrespectfully," they say. "One may not eat or drink in them, nor dress in them, nor stroll about in them, nor go into them in summer to escape the heat and in the rainy season to escape the rain." Some of the later authorities go so far as to rule that it is forbidden for a father to kiss his child in the synagogue so as to avoid any demonstration of human affection in a place dedicated to the worship of God. It is further taught that the synagogue should be well lit and kept perfectly clean. As a token of respect the worshipper should bow towards the ark on entering and leaving the synagogue.

Traditionally, the synagogue fulfils an educational, as well as a devotional, function. It is the house of learning as well as the house of prayer. It is for this reason that such importance is attached to the reading of the Torah during the service on the Sabbaths and Festivals.

> *Now, in these synagogues, prayer, though an essential element of worship, formed only one of its component parts. Instruction in the Law complemented prayer in the order of service. For worship, Jewishly conceived, is the service of the heart, which is prayer, supplemented by the joy of the heart, which is Torah. Accordingly, the synagogal liturgy, we find, is more than a book of prayers; it is essentially a manual of divine worship, comprising many prayers of adoration, thanksgiving, and petition, but abounding likewise in vital religious instruction. Impressive recitals of the salient facts of sacred history and solemn reiterations of the fundamental principles of the faith find their place, alongside of the purely*

> *devotional elements, in the service. And so, too, the reading from the Scroll, with the subsequent interpretation of the passage read, came to form as much a part of worship as the prayers and meditations.*[1]

In short, by setting aside a place in which to worship, by repairing there frequently to replenish his spiritual powers, by learning there what his faith has to teach about life and its meaning, and by meeting there with like-minded fellows to encourage him and to strengthen him in his resolves, the Jew " ascends the mount of the Lord." He comes into contact with a world of elevated values and though he may soon come down to earth again he is the better for having been on the heights.

> *There is much comfort in high hills,*
> *and a great easing of the heart.*
> *We look upon them, and our nature fills*
> *with loftier images from their life apart.*
> *They set our feet on paths of freedom, bent*
> *To snap the circles of our discontent.*

The synagogue can do this for the modern Jew who learns, as his ancestors did, to revere it and make its ideal his own.

---

[1] Israel Bettan: *Studies in Jewish Preaching*, Cincinnati, 1939, p. 5.

www.ingramcontent.com/pod-product-compliance
Lightning Source LLC
LaVergne TN
LVHW020100090426
835510LV00040B/2724